TESTING THE ELEMENTS

TESTING THE ELEMENTS

Bruce Meyer

Library and Archives Canada Cataloguing in Publication

Meyer, Bruce, 1957-, author
      Testing the elements / Bruce Meyer.

Poems.
Issued in print and electronic formats.
ISBN 978-1-55096-393-9 (pbk.) — ISBN 978-1-55096-394-6 (pdf)

      I. Title.

PS8576.E93T47 2014   C811'.54   C2014-900182-7
                                               C2014-900183-5

Design and Composition by Mishi Uroboros
Cover Photograph by Sean Puckett
Typeset in Bodoni SvtyTwo font at Moons of Jupiter Studios

Published by Exile Editions Ltd ~ www.ExileEditions.com
144483 Southgate Road 14 – GD, Holstein, Ontario, N0G 2A0
Printed and Bound in Canada in 2014, by Imprimerie Gauvin

We gratefully acknowledge, for their support toward our publishing
activities, the Canada Council for the Arts, the Government of Canada
through the Canada Book Fund (CBF), the Ontario Arts Council, and
the Ontario Media Development Corporation.

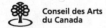

Canadian Sales: The Canadian Manda Group, 165 Dufferin Street,
Toronto ON M6K 3H6 www.mandagroup.com 416 516 0911

North American and International Distribution, and U.S. Sales:
Independent Publishers Group, 814 North Franklin Street,
Chicago IL 60610 www.ipgbook.com toll free: 1 800 888 4741

This book is for
Kerry, Katie, Margaret, and Carolyn

and in memory of friend and mentor
Seamus Heaney

Dawn

i.m. Seamus Heaney, August 30, 2013

Yellow hedgerow gorse blinked and fell
at summer's end on a hill slope waking wet
in dewy blessing. Sun sang in each bauble.
Fields clasped rosaries of ancient starlight.

It is time, sky and humbled clouds rolled on,
for silence to learn the silence of fierce sleep,
to learn the world's living voice alive again
risen from pain to life to love to live in the deep

earthen footprints of fattened flocks grazing
the worried slides. Words are carved on wind
and filter boughs of father oaks phrasing
a spell from what was said and left behind,

never to be forgotten the way a shadow shows
the outline of a body wherever the soul goes.

Contents

Nature, that fram'd us of four elements
Warring within our breast for regiment,
Doth teach us all to have aspiring minds.

> —CHRISTOPHER MARLOWE, *Tamburlaine the Great,*
> *Part One,* II.vii, 17-29

And these Things,
which live by perishing, know you are praising them; transient,
they look to us for deliverance: us, the most transient of all.
They want us to change them, utterly, in our invisible heart,
within – oh endlessly – within us! Whoever we may be at last.

> —RAINER MARIA RILKE, *Ninth Duino Elegy*

The Penguin Book of Mayan Verse

There was a time when time ran out
in the middle of a Wednesday lunch
while crowds cheered for hoops at the stadium
someone said *c'mon, let's go*
and everyone got up and left.

Sentences dangled unfinished in mid-air.
Weaving was abandoned on the looms.
Clocks no longer foretold tomorrows.
Surrounding jungles became dry prose.
Their poetry sat open and unshelved:

villanelles and triolets of Mayan angst,
sestinas patterned in elaborate dances
were reduced to trails of jaguar prints
in places they loved and dreams they knew,
and nothing was left to be learned by heart.

They believed worlds end
in epics of elements
but when they had to pick up and go
much good it did them, much love they left.
Their world fell silent as a rural library.

But someone captured that sacred view
deep in the depths of Chichen Itza,
with a reverence we hold for Chaucer now,
and the reflection always looking back
is reading of joy from a book of hours.

Earth

Forage Caps

in memory of Lt. Arthur Ardagh,
Simcoe Foresters, d. 1917

I

As far as the failing eye can see
in the Niagara Camp panorama,

white tents stretch like brides
parading before their promises.

Front, the photographer's shadow
in the November sun is cast

as if it is the shadow of death
perched on a ladder, admiring

the fire in faces of the men.
There are so many now indistinct,

so far away as to be indistinguishable
as stories someone told long ago

and then forgot. This is the amnesia
history fashions so we can remember.

II

Overseas. Simcoe Foresters. 177.
Each maple leaf plucked

from a tree is autumn gold
where the black branches strain

to hold the light of an exhausted day
that was too short in its own time.

Each body in the ordered ranks
is lithe and trim, each glowing face

bears a ruddiness of living months
outdoors beneath bleached canvas

with the comfort of autumn damp
tucked inside pockets of great coats.

Each one of them, the photo tells us,
is holding his breath – the boy

who crouches in the front row
like a footnote to their discipline;

the square-shouldered man whose brow
is like a second peak above his eyes;

the man who was smiling at something
still standing right behind you,

and the stern officer whose moustache
is composed of two spread arms

that fail to hold on the world in abeyance.
The moment you turn away is history.

III

History is the art of forgetting with style.
It comes with a penchant for details

that cannot explain the truth of things—
the number of dead, lives of the wounded,

shadows of footprints as ranks broke
and the soft ground beneath each boot

shrank and regained its shape, grew
another season and another after that

until there were no more shadows...only
the memory of a moment when men

in forage caps, their badges beaming
in the soft light of a bright afternoon

recorded their presence, telling the world
of their purpose, the way a thousand ships

sailed east into the late day darkness
and were witnessed only by a blind poet

who thought he understood their goal
as his eyes gazed whitely into time.

On the Exhumation of Neruda's Body

What will they find in Neruda's remains?
That he was poisoned by madmen or worse?
He loved the people, championed their claims.

Bodies suffer and die, enduring mortal pains.
The heart breaks and is reborn in due course.
What will they find in Neruda's remains?

The shards of an exile? The brains
of a diplomat? Heart of a lion? A curse?
He loved the people, so history claims.

Poetry is never held prisoner. It complains
whenever it stands still, impatient and terse.
Is there anything left of Neruda's remains?

Death is merely another edition. Soft strains
of moonlit tangos scuffle and rehearse
the dance of love until only love claims

the right to shroud the poet's mortal remains
with death and silence. Only life can write verse.
So what will they find in Neruda's remains?
Love's will? More love? Everything love claims?

Myth

Charles Dickens arrived in Toronto
as the drenched crowd applauded.
Rain shone on our soaked shoulders.
Stories froze in our open mouths.
The day was meant for celebration—
for literature, real literature, had come.
Not backwoods jokes of muddy shoes.
Or dead children beneath draped pines.
Real suffering, something to believe in.
When the moment came for him to speak
the words were disappointing. We'd
heard the sad stories before. The night
was clearing. Constellations bent down
from forever and bit our cheeks
with frank wonder. November stung us.
And we remembered the moment
of our arrival: snow falling helplessly,
and footprints in the brown muck
staking a claim we wanted to call home.

Clean Fill

I

Warmer than a lover's morning touch
and carrying the breath of a newborn day

exhaled from a sleeper's mouth, such
darkness is almost beautiful the way

death is beautiful in its fetid sleep
before it turns an ugly face and brings

forth the kind of life, in failure, deep
memories utter in reborn things.

Put your hands in it, sink them in the proof
that the death of one thing is the life

of something else, and learn to love
the peelings and trailings, the truth

that what is left behind can make for growth.
Is this what you are – that taste in your mouth?

II

When my spade sank in the black mountain
that turned Willow Creek Valley to a hill,

you knew I was retching on the smell,
that tang in my lungs I could not contain.

Beneath me was the sum of local history,
the scents and soup cans that fascinate

a delver troweling, uncertain of date,
but granted the privilege of archeology.

Each spring we return to this compost
outcrop to fill plastic tubs with wastes

of other people's dinners, tasteless tastes
of expired fruits. Let us make the most

of our city's grand decay, seed and prime
our garden with what gardens become in time.

Berczy Park

The rain in Berczy Park is cold tonight.
The trees of Barrie shed brown leaves,
the way history is grown only to perish.
The truth Brant points to remains a secret,
and if you go there you must warn the others.

If the painter, Berczy, is looking north,
Joseph Brant stands on the Grand River
and raises his right index finger westward,
suggesting that memory must move on
just as time and storms and seasons do.

A small yellow hound is paying attention,
its head slightly cocked on behalf of nature—
someone, the canine understands, must listen.
Saplings drop their infant blossoms.
Their ancestor on the ground is dying.

Berczy knew what Brant had survived—
the lost rich soil of the Mohawk Valley,
the hack stump path of American progress,
and too many winters spoken by winds.
If you have ears then you must not hear.

On Brant's neck hangs the King's image,
a red cloak wraps his shirted shoulders,
a shot horn is slung to his torso's right.
His musket butt rests upon the ground
and the hammer is cocked as if ready to fire.

The Remains of Bidwell

You could tell someone had been drinking
when they laid the path of the Irish Road.
Perhaps it was early one summer morning
after a long and inspired August night
and more than a few trees got in the way.
The road was a monologue repeating itself

and stopped when they decided *we must be here.*
There was goldenrod enough to fire a crock,
a shining rainbow that drowned their sorrows,
and the unexpected clock of a lovely lake
where splashing ticked against the shore
and hills in the afternoon spoke prophecy.

But such a place cannot contain itself.
What passes for infectious laughter here
is little more than rocks and amnesia
until those who lived here forgot where they lived
and stumbled somewhere else to die
and doors and rocks looked about the same.

True, there is still the grey and shingled church,
leaning as a matter of faith to the east,
the outline of a clapboard blacksmith's shop
falling apart for want of a nail, its lucky horseshoe
above the door swung so its luck ran out,
and the name on the sign is a dead man's grin.

But think: how many places in this world
wish you well in the course of their name?
And you find yourself here as a matter of pride
knowing whatever brought you is smiling,
and happy, and, unafraid in some hung-over way.

African Methodist Episcopal Church

Follow the trace of rabbit
tracks through brilliant snow.
They disappear into a thicket
as threadbare in February

as strangers in a new land.
Your shadow lengthens.
The sun becomes a clock,
and time sets you against

the brown clapboards,
glass rippling like water
from the day it was made.
The logs are redemption hymns.

Cross cuts are locked together
as if fingers clasped in prayer.
Lord, they call, *deliver us
and we shall build a temple*

*in that holy place where Time
and Eternity meet disguised
as a cross of the 8th concession
and the Old Barrie Road.*

The rabbits trod gently
where you, respectfully,
choose not to walk, the snow
knee-deep and cold as freedom,

and a place in the winter sun
is all the history you can claim,
a footprint melting in the snow,
asking deliverance.

Brown Shoes

for John B. Lee

A man wears brown shoes cautiously
because he doesn't know any better,
because in them he has seized the moment
when the chance for shoes presents itself
and he doesn't care if they match navy
or the shades of blackish grey in suits.

He wears brown shoes defiantly
because he has a fear of undertakers,
fears their dour, hushed-up voices,
does not want his wife to be afraid
of winter Sundays all by herself
or the sound of his chair sitting empty.

And wearing brown shoes too long,
a man believes his moment has come
and dons white shoes for leisure
until the truth of his mortality sinks in
and he remembers his lost grandfather
for whom brown meant a life of work.

A man in comfortable brown shoes
knows they are the colour of earth,
knows a nostalgia for touching the soil
and remembers the strength Antaeus had

when Hercules held his coil aloft
and the giant shrank in the strong arms.

To touch the earth is no laughing matter:
the touch of earth is the need to feel,
a love of springtime, the clutch of mud,
the long-held belief that earth feeds life,
and that no one dies pure of heart
unless he absolves the God of seasons.

A man wears brown shoes with hope
unafraid of mortal simplicities,
understands how time will grip him,
until the dust and the man are one
and the place he stands and his shoes
are of that element that longs for more.

Fox in the Fallen Snow

So we stand at the window
with the question of snow
on our minds and have no
answer. We should know

better. Four feet print the lawn.
Little feet. Something at dawn
that shivers, that cannot go on
but must. It hungers, on and on.

The dog growled in the night;
watched snow in the streetlight
fall perfectly on the white
lawn mussed by the fox's feet.

This is not about printing a page.
This is about what is there: rage,
fear, cold on the neck to engage
death with mere touch, the cage

we live in, the eyes that peer
into the night, into the new year,
the dying year, the time we are
here, watching. The fox is here.

Take up the night as a blanket.
Wrap it around your body, yet
show me your nakedness. Set
love against death. Do not forget.

Water

What's Left of Nineveh

After the visitations and pronouncements
when we were all bone-tired of stones
being turned over to see if sin lay beneath

and the shores where we took our picnics
on bright summer days in happier times
were strewn with the jetsam of failed prophets,

we asked our spirits if any love was left,
envied gentle souls whose rage is grace,
shadows who deceived us with such goodness

we struck a face of awe upon our coins
and spent them as if tomorrow we'd be dead.
We learned to pay the debt that angels bear.

These streets were once beloved, honoured
for the flaws of gods who walked among us
to voice their desires through our imperfections.

Lessons sting. The old ways die hard. Truth
has its price even when it seems a lie. This city,
our Nineveh, is paved with good intentions,

and its streets reach out to meet the world
as rain blesses our rooftops and gutters,
as we outlast the sea to fall again.

Horses

Heraclitis would have said
they were born from snow,
the white ones whose breath
is a cloud dappling the horizon,
a cloud with four legs
that bears the semblance
of a pale paper stallion
imagined as you read this.

They were of the sea.
The Trojans saw mains
in the surf against Asia,
saw the breaking of horses
as the rotting of Greek ropes
during long summer days
when a glow of plankton
shimmered the ocean's skin
and salt clouds of sweat
engulfed castled headlands.

To touch one is to know direction,
a stroke smooth and with the hair
reminds you of the flow
of keel and hull and silence
that fills the sails quietly
until the ribs beat a gallop
in a heart's measure of measures
and the horse becomes a poem.

Ride this with the wind.
There is blood flowing within.
It knows you have reined it,
knows you are holding it
in hands that rank
its stature among horses
as it stares you in the eye
and moves gently toward you
to lap your outstretched palm
and sing the cadence of your voice.

The Narrows

for Jean and Rex Payne

We finished our evening meal
on your dock as the kingfisher came,
striking his orange and lake blue
in a regal sunset.

Once, near here, the Wendat staked
the channel silts for a weir
as the fish ran in a currency of hunger
north to Couchiching.

It was a communion, the word
for thanks, a full belly with winter
coming in dwindling light,
water through fingers.

Kingfisher and I locked stares.
He knew that whatever sluices
between lakes was the ancient ritual
of hospitality, one lake

offering sustenance to the next,
and in the end it is all one lake,
one enormous gulp the Spirit swallows,
a breath after the prayer.

That is why our voices rise
from the narrows of our throats
as someone tells a story or laughs
or tilts a glass of wine.

Musée de Bon Chance

The first gallery is devoted entirely
to mementos of fortunate journeys:
see unused tickets from the *Titanic*.

Lindberg's soft grey rabbit's foot,
the banked colour of Atlantic fog,
is said to help gas tanks run on empty.
.
There is Sir Francis Drake's life vest,
a model of the last ship from Krakatoa,
and a puck a goalie used to score.

Next is a display that pays homage
to serendipitous moments in time—
Louis Pasteur's cold chicken soup,

the collar of the next dog Banting almost used,
a wall dedicated to the Post-It note,
and answers for passing Judgement Day.

But one gallery is most welcoming:
a replica cloakroom from a party,
a man and woman conversing for hours,

ignoring all the talk around them,
a napkin from their first spaghetti lunch,
a flake of snow from the night they kissed.

At the gift shop on the way out
you can purchase a box of heartbeats
and a envelope of powdered love.

Some things are lucky just to be here.
And if we stay to closing, keep the ticket.
It is good tomorrow and every day after.

Loonie

The image on the coin watches over you.
It sits by itself on the quiet lake,
remote and closer to the stars than time
so it sings the lonely sound of reflection.
You are feeling pity for this creature,
its preened regality turned away.
Pity is the emptiness you hear in pines.
It fills the branches and the needles
while smaller birds cock their ears.
This is symbolic of your own heart,
a herald of the sound of rain,
a patter long after the sun has come;
it watches its reflection in brown waters
to admire what it cannot see in itself.

⚹

To admire what it cannot see in itself,
it watches its reflection in brown waters.
A patter long after the sun has come,
a herald of the sound of rain:
this is symbolic of your own heart.
While small birds cock their ears,
it fills the branches and the needles;
pity is the emptiness you hear in pines,
its preened regality turned away—
you are feeling pity for this creature
so it sings the lonely sound of reflection,

remote and closer to the stars than time.
It sits by itself on the quiet lake.
The image on the coin watches over you.

R.M.S. Titanic

The *Titanic* sank the night my grandparents wed.
By candlelight or starlight, love tried to survive.
There are no pictures of either event. Among the dead

we stand, wondering who would come out alive.
It was April at sea, and in Toronto the first blooms
floated on branches. Most family trees thrive

on the adversity of springs cut short too soon.
When the music stopped, silence was passed on
to future generations. They slept in separate rooms,

stopped stories dead in their tracks. It was gone
from plain view quickly, stars shining where music
once lived, the night flowing into a grey dawn,

the inquiries baffled, the legends turned to panic,
and history written. When my uncle died almost
a century later, we were woven into that fabric

of a night, the organist summoning the ghost
of Edwardian bravado with "Nearer My God to Thee,"
as we wheeled the lavish casket out among the last

echoes of love and prayers and starry eternity,
sealing decades with a sprinkling of ash on wave—
our family had no grave save a story buried at sea.

So here is the final closed report opened to prove
that neither ice nor accident were to blame...
and tragedy comes down to silence or love.

Victoria Square

for Katie

The green bronze bust of a hatless soldier
looks bewildered on this January afternoon
as my daughter and I cross Victoria Square.

His round and awe-shot musket ball eyes
are primed with the look of someone who lost
something proud and of great importance

but cannot remember it was ours.
Rain on his epaulets falls like history.
The sky has swallowed our CN Tower.

I wanted to show my daughter the place
where pioneers were once remembered—
four hundred or more bodies – not a trace

among them left on stone; the peasants,
the founders, the defenders, the cursed,
lie beneath us like sleeping tenants

who occupy a basement flat. Katie, know
how your city runs on amnesia, the paths
and tunnels beneath the streets that show

no signs of the life below, places so worth
remembering we keep them secret
and save them in stories and misplaced truths.

Think of the postcards I send of Torontos,
the pictures of buildings shining and bright,
of gold baked in bank tower windows

where we see blurred shadows of ourselves
imposed on Utopias and pristine under glass.
The square's soft earth sticks to our shoes.

The line between madness and hearty
genius is fine as the cables that stretch above,
stories crossing inside our heads, hung heavy

with tiny drops that falling fall and remain alone;
the tears I could cry if only I knew the depth
of days we live, rain-soaked, shivering for home.

The Snowmen

They have vanished before the avarice
and the oppression of the White Man,
as snow before a summer sun. —TECUMSEH

Their lives leave shadows
wherever they once stood,
not histories or legacies,
but a vision that watches us
with the intensity of buttons
through undone buttonholes.
We took away their clothes
as March thaw gave way
to blossoms of forsythia,
and even naked, shivering
beneath stars they remained
and stared at us as we slept.
As the light grows dusty
you can see their outlines
waiting among tiger lilies.
Be careful where you step.
When we planted them,
we inspired the fallen sky.
Will they melt into the landscape?
We cannot say. They were here
before we told ourselves they were.

The Frogs

brekekekex koax hoax —ARISTOPHANES

I

They answer each other this spring night
with a sound that is not of this world
but of the stars and gears of stars
grinding out the crystal mastery of time
among cedar trees wet to their ankles.
They are in love with the moon's machine.
They are praising their own beauty reflected
in a mirror of memory that does not reflect.

Between the starring eyes of headlights
twinned for journeys into nowhere,
they look back at you through darkness
wanting to fall in love with all they touch.
They are singing their song tonight for you,
and you must listen as they mark their time.

II

We pull off the highway in May twilight
as if to push the world back to life by stopping
in the afterglow for ice cream, the summer
dancing in our desires before it learned to walk.

On the soft shoulder of the road where melt
water lingered from a long winter
came the grating we mistook at first for saws
that could have felled an axle-tree of stars.

But we are not like the mysteries that haunt us—
we explain and answer our desires too easily,
mistaking the sweet satisfaction on our lips
for the kiss of life that still sustains our earth;
and yet we paused to honour and listen to it all,
Devonian song our hearts had long ignored.

III

Permit me the better part of nature in myself—
the spring is as much a part of us as the livid night,

and what we hear in the world when it speaks life
remains in us, bleeds with us, echoes, cries,

and will not be denied. I stand in our doorway
as you sleep silently in the voiceless hours,

knowing that each breath you take is for life,
and life itself is a song of praise for stars;

for in the harmonium of life we heard,
though darkness fell upon our ice-cold lips,

the sound of hearts like ours calling out,
the cry of pain and suffering and love and help.

What passes from the world may be forgotten,
but what we cannot save remains part of us.

Fire

Serendipity

The girl in the Tim Hortons' drive-thru
wears a pearl earring set in the ivory
turnings of her lobe;
and you have heard her speak to you
the way an incorporeal angel asks
what it is that you desire.

The girl at the Tim Hortons' drive-thru
is framed by a window on her soul
and as she turns
serene and serenely startled, you try
to reach and touch her invisible hand.
She remains inviolate;

wears her hair wrapped, her dark eyes
shining a splendor of perfect innocence,
for the answer to longing
is the way an artist saw a gold sunrise
reflected on the canvas of her nape
and lit it in her gaze.

The girl in the Tim Hortons' drive-thru
permits you a glimpse of another world
so mysterious behind her
that you know it serves divine sustenance
requiting the spirit and heart of hunger
as if eternal love:

and your eyes meet for a lifetime's instant,
and you grasp her cup of morning kindness,
a brief, truthful warmth,
and desire an awakening deep inside
to carry you through time's perilous thorns
until you thirst for more.

A Bed in Paris

Many great lovers
have slept here.
Beneath duvet covers,
the majesty of their

nights sets the stars
ablaze in a city
where love and hours
of wild electricity

made this a place
of light. In our bed
we wait for the race
of quick and dead

to summon our spirits,
celebrate life's arts,
and catacomb visits
to each other's hearts.

I chart you in whispers.
Our bodies form a stanza;
our voices are vespers
behind drawn organza.

Sunrise on the St. Lawrence

It is spring again in the country of my life.
The sun has just come up over Quebec City
in a land that drinks new days as if more will come
to cure amnesia.

George Elliott Clarke wrote about finding love
within this city's fortified stone walls
but all this, curtains drawn back on time,
is too easily lost.

When Northrop Frye sailed home to Canada
he felt jaws of headlands close like books,
swallowing him as if Jonah, all the way down
to port at Sorel.

I want to put out an open call for chroniclers,
not poets, and ask that someone make sense
of what we say: not the temple prophet but
the patient scribe.

Patience is easily lost in the name of culture,
patience to hear birdsong in the machinery
of hotel ductwork, a symphony in the gravel crusher
and speak critically

so that love in the name of poetry and poetry
for all the love in sunrises does not vanish from memory
as the miraculous light vanished to the east hours ago
and became poetry.

Welcome to a nation of silence. We speak it beautifully.
The silence of our hearts is the real secret we keep,
swallowed like stones by prophets to keep them from rising
to the light.

Volta

My father would stick metal skewers
into live electrical sockets to feel

if the shock was living. For hours
he would clock thunderstorms, tell

how far away a bolt of lightning struck,
and calculate the number of dinners

it could cook. He glowed pure luck,
a know-how – a shock for beginners.

O! But the brave leave nothing to chance.
A tiny spark was his acrobat leaping

from one point to another, the blue dance
of miraculous energy that was sleeping

the way a horse waits for a leather halter
or fire from Prometheus on a god's altar.

Campagna

In seventeenth-century sketches
when the weather is like today's
and we are out for a long walk
unnoticed by farmers who just sowed
fields with a sacrifice for the sun,
an angel could walk up to us,
his head radiating with heavenly fire
and start a conversation about
the season and the return of green
to the roll of newly planted fields.
Nearby, cows will be lowing.
They will shift from foot to foot
astounded in their shadows that we
should be chosen for a visitation
the way one chooses a loaf of bread
or a bottle of water at a corner store.
And as we stand there sipping
and conversing in a country manner
with a presence that knows so much
and always says so little when asked,
we come to the grand universal truths
burning inside us with such passion
that we cannot utter a single word.
And just when it seems the beauty
of understanding is within our grasp,
I will notice a flock of blackbirds

darting low over the seeded field
and will be astounded such energy
shines on us disguised as life,
and the clouds are aflame with dusk.

The Cayuga

As they broke her up at Sherbourne dock
my grandfather watched and wept. Her hull
torn open exposed the cabins and halls,
pouring sunlight onto a winter day. The shock

of seeing the past ripped from stem to stern
and the glare of the acetylene burn
in the cutter's torch recalled starlight
and the billows of coal smoke in twilight

flowing like the fall of his lover's hair,
how they clung to the railing to watch
Niagara disappear, and homeward to catch
the fire in a sunset and ink in the eastern air.

The Falls and back in a day, the friends,
starlight, the bandshell, the moon's fall
into the grey-veiled afterglow, and all
the bright faces like candles as day ends.

The stacks removed, her wheelhouse torn
for salvage of what could not be saved, a shadow
on the grinning future whose face was worn
smooth by anticipation and the constant flow

of breath woven into fragments of forever;
the young man who was once a young lover,
saw the end of journeys in a welder's spark
the way stars fall when their lives are over.

Sincere

My father's
hands were waxen
and lay folded

with the peacefulness
of extinguished candles.
He was always sincere.

And when my nose
was broken in a game,
I thought the doctor

would patch it up
as if an antique bust
brought back to life

by a team of worker bees.
Or Voltaire's effigy
in Madame Tussaud's,

his eyes almost afire,
almost to the melting,
to wipe out evil things—

sinister things far below,
holding in a dungeon
a Sleeping Beauty

whose stomach rose
and fell with every
breath as delicate

as translucent wings
the sun illumines
the nearer you get to heaven.

The Devil's Paintbrush

The lone weed on the front lawn
is defiant because it wants
to paint the sky the colour of rage.

The lone weed on the front lawn
has a stem like a long spoon
and at the end it tastes of fire,

artist's fire tipped in orange
as if to warn away the faithful.
Brimstone has no place in gardens.

The lone weed on the front lawn
is symbolic of great imperfection.
In the morning shadow of the house

shadows of other worlds gather.
They plot the way things should be,
the colour of the sky becoming

the colour the sky could be painted
if only the brush stem was longer,
if only it could be dipped in fire.

The lone weed on the front lawn
grows in the failure that is art
and reaches to touch the light of God

because it seeks forgiveness for its will,
an artist's will to make the world
a place as new as eternal mornings

when the canvas was a simple question.
The lone weed on the front lawn
seeks the purity of a world redeemed,

desires to be loved and unforsaken,
the sinner rising from sandy soil
the way a pillar of fire shines its light,

God's compass in a sea of sand
slowly guiding the faithful home.
For the lone weed in the front yard

is the brush with which the holy paint
the faces of saints and promised lands
where every plant is good and right

and none are denied the heart's grace
for growing tall and upright toward the Lord,
for the Lord loves all things with His holy fire.

The Lovely Fallen Angels

You should have seen their angelic faces
as they lay in prams and smiled toward
the gangs that lurk in public places—

little bald heads emitting music that graces
postage stamps of butterflies, divinity heard:
you should have seen their angelic faces.

Somewhere in that narrative evil replaces
virtue. I got too close one day. I overheard
the gangs that lurk in public places,

spewing their wrath against God and races
other than theirs. They defiled the holy word;
but they still had such angelic faces

as they broke my nose and ribs, commonplaces
caught on security cameras with those absurd
youths, nightmares who haunt public places.

Neither angelic nor human, idiot joy erases
their lost beauty, so I scream through my blood:
(*and you should have seen their angelic faces*)
burn, you fuckers, who lurk in public places.

Air

Prom Night

The dance continues. The rain speaks.
Suddenly, you stare at your lawn
in the silence of breath you've held
like a mortgage for forty years.
Your life is soaked in spring rain.
You measure time by what little time
you had to accomplish so very little.
There are other loves now, more true,
other rainy nights more meaningful;

she passed through you like a ghost,
leaving her pain and doubt in petals
she dropped from her orchid corsage
as she turned away from your kiss.
Yet you felt a pulse more than your own
and raced against the chimes at midnight
without the map you thought you'd have.
Slowly, the rain leaves the air to ice,
and the open window frames your life.

Underwood

I

Opening the square black suitcase,
I found a thicket frozen in time.

Clustered yellow leaves had fallen
and lay in a wreath of promises.

One leaf may have been intended
for a song or poem to express his love,

for in the detritus of decaying years
I thought I could find a missing word

clacking and rattling among keys,
as a bell sounded. A miracle occurred.

II

He is walking down a windy street.
A broad-brimmed hat and trench coat

tell me he is a man of style, one who
writes his thoughts in little whispers

and passes them to the one he loves.
He sees her on the street ahead, and

with a sudden gasp begins to call her
as she crosses, but a motor drowns her

name. There is silence, an empty space
waiting on the page for time to fill.

No one can complete those lines now.
The period is broken. It can't end this way.

The Prisoner Dreams

How many men do you think would believe themselves
almost in heaven if they possessed even the smallest part
of the luck you still enjoy? This very place which is
banishment to you is home to those who live here.
—BOETHIUS, *The Consolation of Philosophy, Book II*

I

The last dilapidated south wall
of the old Canada West Prison
is crumbling brick by brick.
By night artistic vandals come
with messages for ghostly inmates
and tag their puny, futile claims
that pass with time and world
when all the walls are gone.
Once the largest penitentiary
north of the American border,
lake winds haunted it to dust;
chilled men with mortal visions
of homes and wives forever lost,
a great hall where gallows stood
and the chapel eaten by streets
are no longer monuments to law.
The law laid down its code and slept,
and sentences pronounced in stone
were written in a language lost.
Even after the demolition,
time's choked vocabulary spoke:

remains of hell as raw as February
where damp did its time in chains.
Believe there shall come a time
when walls become archaic dreams
and the peaceable kingdom reigns
indifferent to all human needs;
until then Arthur Ellis' noose
waits the way a window waits
for the impatient to peer through,
knowing such opportunity closes
like daylight on a waking dream.

II

To come by history the way
one comes by souvenirs lying
beneath a barbed-wire fence
is to understand the plight of birds;
caged ones with warmth and food,
enough water to keep a song alive
and if near enough a window
thoughts of what the sky is like,
how vast it is, and how to fear it.
To be free is to struggle always,
to pay the mortgage on open sky,
to feel the chill inside feathers,
the old touch of ancient kin.
To be free is to educate oneself
in the laws of conscience and fear,

to know that what has eaten eats,
and has nothing to hold on to.
There is a pleasure, though,
in walls, that space demarcated
with desire and its gloomy peace,
the loveless hallways drafty
in the morning light, the room
never big enough for dreaming.
Sentence by sentence this is history
and what is bequeathed to prisoners
of their own time and place are keys,
and room upon room remaining
to be built as a heavenly kingdom
in the thoughts; for in this place
are many mansions of the heart
and all may enter to merely wait
as the sound of a gaoler's boney ring
paces the tick of redemption's clock.

The Sweetness

Moonstruck on a bright March night,
fields laid as lunar of their snow
as the orb's running rabbit, a sweetness
hangs there, its shadow in the nose.

This pungency is the promise of spring.
The musky offal that blows townward
until the streets remind me how little
boundary there is between farmlands

and sidewalks dressed in false starlight.
Rabbit is running through the trees,
first, as a frightened dart of light then
outlined and printed in fractured glint

of sap droplets sweating from maples.
My country is alive again. The sweetness,
the steam of candied air on frost,
curls from a sugar shack's hot breath.

Cezanne's Card Players

for Seán Virgo

Watching their hands they say so much,
sizing the look in the other's eyes,
a steadiness of bluff or certainty—
players who do this every afternoon
and have known each other too well,
too long.

Familiarity breeds both contempt and love,
that one always plays a jack against an ace,
that one will lick his thumb to play a heart,
and the other will sigh and scratch his head.
This is the beauty of being reasonable.
This is the patience of art and life
and shadows of light.

Paintings are full of noises.
Out of frame the barmaid can be heard
chatting up a travelling parfumier
whose case of powerful Parisian scents
jingles as he opens the mahogany box
and thinks of new ways he can provide
to simply say hello.

And what they don't say is equally true
and sound as loudly as squat shot glasses
being filled with amber cognac—

the subtle streaming sounds of liquid
coursing through a brook on a spring morning
announcing the voice of life to the world
as if it had never done so before
and may never do so again.

Birds choir their thatch of desires
as they claim their space in the narrow eaves
and an old woman waiting patiently
whispers under her breath
that he ought to play his heart.

Syllabub

The devil has a curriculum for dessert.
He has furnished it with a sweetness
to entice the humours into revel,
and once in disarray, all is misrule.

Cream is purity tainted with temptation.
The good should know better what entices:
sugar, some shrivelled fruit, and *sille*
stolen from a priest's table, and cake

swept from the tongue's touch of spirit.
Prepare the soul. The battle is waged
upon the field of *no* in a world where *yes*
is the final grace after a blessed meal.

Syllabub has been loosed from adamant.
He wants men about him who are fat.

A Lifetime

No one is sure how anything began
or certain of how or when it ends,
but to say it belongs to the person named
is to be gravely mistaken. Stay in bed
for a morning. The telephone keeps ringing.
The emails flood in. To die is to be behind,
behind, to be needed and called and called on
incessantly. To live is to live for others.
The needs of others. Listen to morning rain.
The birds are singing. They are singing
to other birds. They answer note for note.
The others sing back. They are writing
poems about the windows you have left open.
A storm is approaching. They know it.
They are singing songs of a flooded house.
They are singing about the house you own
because others need to live in it. You are
called on by the others to air out the rooms
after the rain has passed and the day is fresh.
This is a new beginning, you say.
But the air rushes in to claim the lungs.
Air on which a lone balloon rides. It floats
past the window you just closed for rain.
The air would carry the balloon to places
stretched rubber skin has only dreamed of,
places the balloon might not want to go,
but has to go because air lives for others.
It is a cool, gentle morning breeze. It blows softly.

It owns the balloon because it loves it.
No one knows where the balloon will land.
It is just its lifetime. Get on with the morning.

The Modern American Poem

The movie star has dropped to the floor
and as she lies there, drug addled,
she experiences a vision of God or truth.

A small creature is suffering. Nature
is horribly cruel not justly indifferent.
The world's mercy collapses in reversal.

A wrist or wounded heart is bleeding.
The pain is about beauty. The horror
is from a parent who was a real shit.

In the heat of a multicultural suburb
a child learns the true meaning of life
and everyone is expected to feel pity.

No first steps on the moon. No cries
of a girl burning from a napalm attack,
and the sound of high jets is secret.

No forgiveness from an apple blossom
that tried its best to outlast the rain.
Shut up. The man with the gun is talking.

Are you waiting to hear about a highway
and the dawn that keeps on driving
until figures beneath a bridge have coughed?

Put this in a wrapper, heat it, and serve it.
Save it for later. What passes for hunger
is the sound of wind in wait for a bird.

Writing on Your Back

The shape of what we say
we learn to feel:

secret messages
fingers scribe
when we stand
beside each other
at fashionable parties—

a glass in one hand,
the other free upon our backs,
our skins as tablets,
our hands pens,

each letter drawn by touch
in the ladder
between our wings.

Listen carefully
as we would to angels
flying up and down our spines—

we have only each other's hearts
to comprehend
and the silence of warm fingers
upon a shivering page.

The Movie Being Filmed
Across the Street

On the Judgement of Dogs

for James Clarke

Don't imagine they get off easy
the way other animals pass
from life to death and beyond—

they have been complicit
in the light and shadows of man,
needing and needed, unquestioning.

Teething-chews on a chair rung,
the theft of a dirty tennis sock,
or the stolen bite of table food

is not enough to weigh a soul;
but the depth and trust in eyes
betray a patience and obligation

that casts, times seven, sins in stone.
Hitler's shepherd comes to mind.
She loved someone and chose badly,

her paws begging for affection;
nature said love and she obeyed.
Her heart knew the concrete bunker,

the clatter of typewriters, caged men,
cries of children being put to sleep,
gates locked forbidding the outside.

In Elysian fields of the heart's reward
she knew she was running toward a ball,
its brilliant light, her mouth open,

a soul racing, and lungs panting;
she craved the sound of her master's voice
growing darker until all was black.

God wrote the Nuremburg laws.
Blondi was simply following orders,
mistaking attention for love itself.

What say you in the case of Blondi?
Is she a victim of the need to obey?
She will come for judgement when you call.

Dreaming of Joe Weider (1920-2013)

I

When nature drew me as a stick boy
easily snapped by neighbourhood bullies,

I wanted to grow strong and fight back
the way the ninety-eight-pound weakling

at the beach was transformed, transfigured,
into a Hercules of he-man stature.

I prayed at the altar of Joe Weider,
slept with the comic-book ad by my pillow,

and saved a dollar for his catalogue.
When I grew old enough to clip the bastards

and strong enough to snap their fucking necks,
I could not bring myself to desire the girl

who hung on the arms of empty-headed men,
so I wrote poems such as this to curse them.

II

When I heard my bones break softly
or my punched gut scream without answer,

I knew that victory would soon be mine.
One bully did twenty years. Another died

at the hands of someone stronger. Another
drank himself to death in a city alley,

his frozen body broken by his own fight.
I am still a weakling yet forgive them now;

the fight's no longer fair. Time stole
the beauty from their sneering girlfriends,

and life simply did the rest. They are
forgotten or so I choose to believe,

but if heaven has a special place for bullies,
I pray their jailer will be stronger too.

In Defence of Narrators

for Marty Gervais

They set the tone, theme, and draw us in.
They know how the story will end
and for them badly as they disappear,
always without their voice to explain,
to tell it the way it ought to be told,
the unmasked truth we really deserve.
They begin the story knowing their part,
sacrifices dead on the cutting room floor.
Partway through they are put to silence.
We listen. The story rattles on by itself.
What if we love and truly need them?
What if they have lovely families to feed?
What if they are neighbours or our friends?
Sometimes their departures are heard.
Sometimes, but rarely, they say goodbye.
Some aspire to be a good Greek chorus,
yearn to describe and react to action,
a character whose cause we undertake,
whose life is important and matters much:
they speak not to us but for and of us.
My great-aunt used to tell me stories
and she never died in a single one,
her tea cup gradually emptying to leaves,
her prophecies certain, her ends her own.
In the movie of my mind I hear her still.
I let her keep talking: I want her to live.

As the credits crawl to the top to die
the narrator's absence causes me grief.
I want to find him and bring him home.
I want him to know we need and love him.
I want to hear his sonorous voice.
I desire justice and the survival of good.
I want truth I can live with and nothing but.
I want a story to vanquish death.
I want a story about the death of death.
I want the story to stop all the clocks
and clocks to tell time without any end.
Narratives are timeless. Let the narrators live.
Let them be blessed. Just let them speak.

Homage to Charles Darwin

Everything changes sometimes for the better.
Ask my dog if this is true. She cocks her ear.
More than anything she wants an opposable thumb.
How about a job where I can become someone?
And could the neurotic chickadees at the feeder
chew their food, as the sun's morning ease
illuminates their fragile angelic wings?
Why do they natter when a wild canary sings?

I look for the impossible in everything I see.
As a boy with twig legs and knobbly knees,
bullies beat me up. I had no excuses, no defence.
I grew big. I could crush them now. I have more sense.
They have families and lives and homes to protect.
Each day I keep my wrath a dark, ancient, secret.

Winter sun is glowing on the page as I write this.
My pen casts a shadow the way a smile or kiss
from my wife tells me there is hope for love among us.
I want to believe her. Sometimes everything changes.
In my next life I will look into men's souls,
they into mine as we fail the way everything fails,
or succeed the way everything wants to succeed, cramped
for food and time and lives nature has stamped
with the seal of approval, an emblem of bitter distrust,
the suspicion of ancestors: *Do well. Do better. Do best.*

Mammoth Skull, Simcoe County Museum

Behold, the light of God is with us now.
The November sky remains an open Psalter.

In blessed paths of iridescent hummingbirds,
other tusks nudged him. He did not answer.

And while the world sang its silent offices,
ocular sockets became transept windows.

Through those eyes, it forgot how to weep.
In his brain, when light finally shone,

Time devoured thought, building a house of God,
a velvet-soft sanctuary of sacrificial moss

as foliage crept over him in golden hymns.
His great weight fell and awaited resurrection.

Superstitions

I

Never leave a notebook open.
Ideas have wandered into the snow

to die and you coax them back
with the warmth of sunlight

to thaw themselves by your hand.
They have been dead a long time

and they do not look well. They
sneer at you through taunt diction

that might have touched the heart.
Open notebooks bleed eulogies.

II

Never leave a pen uncapped.
An empty room is a thirsty place.

The vampire behind the bookshelf
will emerge to drink the reservoir dry.

Or maybe angels take their portion.
Think of words you might have had.

Think of lines that have no ending,
thoughts that disappear like snow.

The sharpness of the nib is blunted.
Nothing is left with which to fight.

III

Never stare too long at an empty page.
The page is bright and contains the sun.

There are wonders one is meant to see
and things that demand the eyes avert.

There are places other minds have gone,
and going were never seen again.

They are out there on that empty page,
sailing blindly in search of home.

Let them figure it out all by themselves.
The page is yours. You made this world.

Matrimony

for Sarah and Michael, 01.06.13

The heart of the matter
is the truth you find in it,
the truth of early winter wakings
when the room is cold
and a touch of hands
redeems the world from darkness.

The heart of the matter
is the truth you bring to it;
the art of finding oneself in another—
something more than ancient poets
beholding their reflection in a beloved's eye,
the soul of the other
who whispers to your ways
in a language that has no words.

The heart of the matter
is in the words you exchange
going and coming at each day's ends,
or the final syllables spoken at night
before you go to encounter your dreams.

The heart of the matter
finds you in a maze,

shivering against the Minotaur's rage,
so take each other as valiant survivors
to places where dreams are never lost—

the way two people are meant to meet,
and know your lives are a golden thread
knotted around the door to hope.
For the heart of the matter
is the heart itself,
the knot a love knot never undone.
What it seals and what it becomes
is a mystery you will solve together.

The Movie Being Filmed Across the Street from My Hotel Window

We are always somewhere else in our dreams.
Somewhere in a moment that is not ours.
The director motions the figures to marks.
The extras are arranged in arrayed tableaux.
I search for allegories in the way they stand,
the way the faithful might have been depicted
in an illuminated medieval triptych,
their eyes solemn and focused with devotion,
a bright light shaping the shadows of their faces.

The director charges them with their duties—
self-abandonment,
the obligation to relinquish their inner lives,
to become someone else,
someone nameless in a crowd,
someone totally unlike themselves.

And because we are always elsewhere in our dreams
this is not the city at the end of dreams,
because the real New York of concrete and exhaust
is hundreds of miles away to the east
and it is warm there on this new spring night,
the buds are opening in Central Park,
and the New York smell of sea and cigarettes
hangs in the air the way trees perfume
after rain has fallen and the streetlamps reflect.

And the supplicants spread their lives on a platter
because they are martyrs to the silence of new lives
and believe their rebirth is close at hand,
labour with the intensity of true believers:
they are pilgrims who have arrived at a shrine
and stand patiently waiting for a miracle to happen,
for their eyes to be opened and something wonderful to be named.

This is not eternity but the idea of forever.
Life wants everyone to aspire to greatness.
The breath of the crowd the director imagines
is a chronicle of life halted in retelling,
still and motionless beneath my window
and the road to stillness is paved in snow.
The lights of the NYPD cruisers
are flashing beacons of tabernacle lamps
alarming the city of living souls
that the dawn will soon invade desires.

No place remains for the mind to go
except the street where it has always been,
a view from a window on a world asleep,
still-life framed by pixilated frame
that is not the street but the image in the word:

for we are always somewhere else in our dreams
where snowflakes stand in as falling petals
to prove what is here and now and is not true
is the surety of heaven within ourselves,
the loss of the self that must find the self,
and know we can reach it if only in our dreams.

Moonlight on Sleepers

In Claude Lorrain's *The Ford*,
moonlight greets the shepherds
as they cross the glistening stream,
amplifying their shadowed features

as if spectres whose visible souls
are on the way to their redemption.
Their faces are etched landscapes
and eternity is a map they follow

the way no words can ever praise
the shadows that refine your body
into the mysteries of lost continents
with moonlight through our window.

I will not wake you to tell you now
just how beautiful you are in moments
when I am apt to know it least.
I'll describe it better on the other side.

Scan the QR to enjoy a video
of Bruce Meyer reading two poems.
Or access via URL at:
www.tinyurl.com/ClarkeTraverse

(4:40)

ACKNOWLEDGEMENTS

The author is grateful to the following journals for the previous publication of several of the poems in this collection:

"Clean Fill," *University of Windsor Review*

"The Narrows," *The Warwick Review* (UK)

"Invisible Snowmen," *Sulphur* (appears in this volume as "The Snowmen")

"Victoria Square," *An Unfinished War*, ed. John B. Lee (Black Moss Press)

"Horses," "The Remains of Bidwell," "Cezanne's Card Players," "Serendipity," "On the Exhumation of Neruda's Body," "Myth," "Fox in the Fallen Snow," "What's Left of Nineveh," were part of a suite, *Horses and other poems*, long-listed for the $2,500 Gwendolyn MacEwen Poetry Competition. "The Prisoner Dreams," "On the Judgement of Dogs," "The Movie Being Filmed Across the Street from My Hotel Window," and "Dreaming of Joe Weider," were part of a suite, *Moonshell and other poems*, long-listed for the same prize.

"Cezanne's Card Players" and "The Movie Being Filmed Across the Street from My Hotel Window" were shortlisted for the Best Single Poem category of the $2,500 Gwendolyn MacEwen Poetry Competition.

The author would like to thank the following individuals or institutions for their support, encouragement, and kindness in the process behind this book: Michael Hulse of the University of Warwick; The Grey and Simcoe Foresters Museum of Barrie, Ontario; Mariella Rowan of the Grey and Simcoe Foresters Honorable Guard; the staff of the National Gallery of Canada, Ottawa; H. Masud Taj; John B. Lee; Rudi Quammie Williams and the Department of Culture, City of Barrie; John Wing; Jean and Rex Payne of Orillia, Ontario; James Clarke; George Elliott Clarke; Marty Gervais; Fiona Pitt-Kethley; the staff of the Simcoe County Museum, Midhurst, Ontario; Mary Louis Sulcs; Michael Schellenberg and Helen Floros; Halli Villegas; CKUA Radio, Edmonton Alberta; Bob Chelmak; Brian Dunsmore; Dr. Norman Cornett and his students in the Dialogic Serminars in Montreal. Thanks to Karen Wetmore and the staff of Grenville Printing at Georgian College for their kindness throughout this project.

The author is grateful to the Ontario Arts Council Writers' Reserve Program and the Ontario Arts Council Works-in-Progress Program for their support of this project.

A very special thanks goes to Barry Callaghan, Michael Callaghan, Gabriela Campos, and Nina Callaghan of Exile Editions for their continued belief in my work; and to my editor on this project, Sean Virgo, whose command of ideas and expression, keen ear, and masterful sense of language challenged me to learn more and think more about my work.

And, as always, my appreciation to Kerry, Katie, Margaret, and Carolyn, and my constant companion, Daisy.

About the Author

Bruce Meyer is author of numerous books of poetry, short fiction, non-fiction, and pedagogy. His most recent works from Exile are *Alphabestiary: A Poetry Emblem Book* (with H. Masud Taj), *A Book of Bread*, and the new edition of *We Wasn't Pals: Canadian Poetry and Prose of the First World War* (co-edited with Barry Callaghan with an Afterword by Margaret Atwood). He is professor of English at Georgian College in Barrie, Ontario, Victoria College at the University of Toronto, St. Michael's College Continuing Education Program at the University of Toronto, and Laurentian University's B.A. Program in Barrie. He is the inaugural Poet Laureate of the City of Barrie.

BRUCE MEYER BOOKS WITH EXILE EDITIONS

Poetry

Anywhere (2000)

The Spirit Bride (2002)

Oceans (2004)

Alphabestiary: A Poetry Emblem Book
  (with H. Masud Taj; 2011)

A Book of Bread: Poems (2012)

Testing the Elements (2014)

Works edited

Selected Poems of Frank Prewett
  (with Barry Callaghan, 1987)

We Wasn't Pals: Canadian Poetry and Prose of the
  First World War
  (with Barry Callaghan, with an Afterword by
Margaret Atwood, 2000; New Edition, 2014)

Selected Poems of Frank Prewett
  (with Barry Callaghan, Pica Edition, 2000)

James Hanley, *The German Prisoner: A Reflection of*
  Those Unspoken Times During the First World War
  (2006)

a book of
Bread

poems

Bruce Meyer

ALPHABESTIARY

A POETRY~EMBLEM BOOK

H. Masud Taj

AND

Bruce Meyer